HOW TO TALK YOUR WAY

OUT OF A

TRAFFIC TICKET

BY

DAVID W. KELLEY
Highway Patrolman

Illustrated by PAUL MICHAEL DAVIES

CCC PUBLICATIONS • LOS ANGELES

Published by

CCC Publications
21630 Lassen St.
Chatsworth, CA 91311

Manufactured in the United States of America

Cover design © 1989 CCC Publications

Cover Art by Michael Cressy

Cover Production by The Creative Place

Illustrations by Paul Michael Davies

Illustrations © 1989 David Kelley & CCC Publications

ISBN: 0-918259-21-5

If your local U.S. bookstore is out of stock, copies of this book may be obtained by mailing check or money order for $4.95 per book (plus $2.50 to cover postage and handling) to: CCC Publications; 21630 Lassen Street, Chatsworth, CA 91311.

Pre-Publication Edition November 1989
First Edition February 1990
Third printing — August 1990
Fourth printing — February 1991
Fifth printing — May 1991
Sixth printing — August 1991
Seventh printing — November 1991
Eighth printing — May 1992

TABLE OF CONTENTS

DEDICATION

This book is dedicated to you, the general motoring public, for being the good people that you are and for the cooperation and support I have personally received from you over the years (with a few minor exceptions). To my wife, Mary, who supported me in writing this book and in everything I do. To my youngest son, Dennis, for the original illustration concepts (when I could get him away from his girlfriend). And to my oldest son, David, who has received so many tickets that I became inspired to write this book.

ABOUT THE AUTHOR

David Kelley has been a California Highway Patrolman for over twenty-three years. Prior to becoming a Highway Patrolman, he spent three years serving with a city police department in Southern California. He is still with the Highway Patrol, assigned to an office in Northern California, and still actively engaged in accident investigations and enforcing traffic laws.

He says, "In my twenty-six years of experience I have dealt with a wide variety of people with many different personalities. I have discovered that:

A) Many people have never been stopped by the police before.

B) Many people who have been stopped really didn't know how to respond. Nor did they know how to act in order to make their brief encounter with the police as easy and positive an experience as possible. And,

C) **That if more people had some guidelines as to how to deal with and talk to the police—along with a better understanding of how police officers think—in *many* cases it *is* possible to "TALK YOUR WAY OUT OF A TRAFFIC TICKET."**

Officer Kelley felt there was a need to make this information available to the public. This book, based on his experience and training, is a *must* for anyone who drives a car!!!

ARE YOU READY FOR THIS?

4

SURPRISE

You are driving along, minding you own business, listening to your favorite music on the car stereo. Your mind is anywhere but on your driving. You are thinking about a football game—about your next vacation—what to fix for dinner when your husband comes home from work—or that you are going to be late for an appointment!

Suddenly, something is wrong. You feel uneasy. What is it? There seems to be a red glow coming from somewhere. There is a startling, high-pitched noise coming from behind you. Immediately your mind returns to your driving. You look in the rear-view mirror. Oh no! A police car! It's lit up like a Christmas Tree and it's after YOU! Your eyes move quickly to the speedometer. Damn! Fifteen miles an hour over the speed limit. Your foot comes off the gas pedal so fast your leg almost cramps. Your heart starts beating faster. Your mind suddenly becomes very active. As you slow down and pull over to the side of the road you are trying to think of what to say. Maybe if you don't come to a stop too quickly, you will have a little more time to gain your composure and come up with a good story?

How can you get out of this? You don't want a ticket. You don't *need* a ticket! This could cost you some money. Your insurance rates will probably go up—or your insurance could be cancelled! You think, "I really wasn't going that fast—can I talk my way out of this?" But, what in the world could you possibly say? How should you act? Should you act angry and try to put the cop on the defensive? Should you act self-righteous so the officer will think you don't deserve a ticket? Should you play down the significance of your speed? After all, everyone drives over 55, right? Look at that other guy—he has to be speeding—so why me?

In your rear view mirror you see the officer getting out of his patrol car and approaching your vehicle. Panic sets in. Perhaps you already have received two or three tickets because you did everything wrong after you were stopped. Maybe you have never been stopped and you don't have the slightest idea what to say or how to act. Maybe every time you are stopped you end up in jail but still can't figure out exactly why. One thing is sure—you know you are in trouble—and you wish there was someone to quickly give you some advice...

Maybe I can help.

COMMUNICATION IS THE KEY!!!

The most important thing you need to know at this point is how to communicate with the officer after you have been pulled over to the side of the road. The contact between you and the person behind the badge can be relatively pleasant or very unpleasant depending primarily on the ability of the two parties involved to communicate with each other. Your ability to talk your way out of a ticket can be enhanced with a better understanding of the duties and a personal perspective of the police officer. That's what this book is all about: *human relations—communication*—and finally, something I can't stress enough, *ATTITUDE!!!*

INTRODUCTION

Most people think getting stopped by the police is an intimidating situation. But it doesn't have to be. Talking your way out of a traffic ticket can actually be fun—or challenging. If you apply the secrets I'm going to share with you, the possibilities are unlimited.

You can impress all your friends and relatives with the story of how you just talked your way out of a ticket. Think of the cop who just arrived home from work and it finally dawns on him that you used some tricky psychology on him and cheated him out of a ticket. Think of all the money you will save in fines, attorney fees and insurance costs. How can you lose?

*   *   *

I have attempted to make the information in this book generalized enough that it should apply almost anywhere. However, if any of the information within these pages conflicts with any policies or procedures used by the police within your area or state, by all means abide by your own local laws and regulations.

This book is intended to be a general guide in a human sense and not in a legal sense. It provides you with information that you can use to put the odds more in your favor when attempting to avoid the unpleasant experience of receiving a traffic ticket.

[NOTE: I would like to emphasize in the beginning that if you are confronted with a SERIOUS legal problem and need legal advice, this information will probably not be helpful. You may need to consult with an attorney.]

A point needs to be made at the outset. There is only one way to guarantee "beating" a traffic ticket. That is to obey all traffic laws so as not to be stopped by the police in the first place. However, the courts and the police recognize that it is difficult, if not impossible, to obey all traffic laws at all times, even if you are trying to do so. For instance, who can anticipate a sudden burned out tail lamp or headlight? *[NOTE: This is known as an "equipment violation" and may result in a regular ticket and a fine or only a "warning ticket". In either case, the usual procedure is, you have the malfunction fixed immediately, then demonstrate to a police officer that you have complied. He signs the ticket and you send it in to the court.]*

* * *

In writing this book, I have intended to offer suggestions relating to your attitude and actions which, during your confrontation with the officer, might keep him or her from writing that ticket.

Depending upon the severity of the violation itself, what you are thinking, how you react and what you say will have an important effect—and, in some cases, will probably be the determining factor as to whether or not you receive a ticket.

SO WHAT'S YOUR PROBLEM, COP?
TRYING TO MAKE YOUR QUOTA?

ATTITUDE

Okay, the red light has come on and you are now pulled over to the curb waiting for the officer to arrive at your window, ticket book in hand...

Perhaps you think the police are a necessary evil—or an unnecessary evil. You may be thinking that if it were not for the police, we would *all* be in trouble—or that if it weren't for the police, *you* wouldn't have any troubles.

What you think doesn't matter at this point. All you need to know now is how do you get out of this ticket?

POLICE ARE PEOPLE TOO

Since we are talking about traffic tickets in a human sense, let's start with the policeman or policewoman, whichever the case may be.

First of all, contrary to common belief, policemen are human. Honest! They really are! Take a look. Many, before they joined the force, have been truck drivers, plumbers, carpenters, factory workers, etc. They have educations ranging from high school graduates to those with college Masters Degrees. Most are married, have children, have hobbies and in general have the same hopes and problems in dealing with life as anyone else.

The reason for pointing out that police are just other human beings is to show that many times their decisions are based on normal human reactions, emotions and inter-relations—and not as much on strict adherence to departmental policies as you might think.

TRAFFIC LAWS—ULTIMATELY FOR YOUR BENEFIT

Another thing to keep in mind is that a traffic officer is merely enforcing laws that citizens, such as yourself, have requested or demanded or caused to be enacted over the years to keep traffic flowing smoothly and safely. The idea is that we may all reach our destinations with a minimum of delays or injuries in a world crowded with automobiles.

Also, investigations by the police into traffic collisions have, in many cases, uncovered a need to establish new laws or guidelines for driving in order to reduce or eliminate the possibility of future injuries or death.

Every time you or someone you know is directly affected by the irresponsible act of another driver on the highway, you probably feel the need for some kind of immediate corrective or punitive action to be taken against that other careless driver. The police are, after all, just another citizen we are paying to help us and protect us from the irresponsible and often malicious acts of others. But, when you see the red light flashing in *your* rear-view mirror and realize he's after *you*, it's probably hard to see things this way and empathize with *his* job.

14

YOUR FRAME OF MIND...

Well, there you are sitting at the curb watching in your mirror for the policeman to get out of his car and approach you. What is your frame of mind right now?

A. It could be *anger* if you are in a hurry and don't want to be delayed.

B. It could also be *injustice* if you feel you have done nothing wrong.

C. It could be *fear* if you have never been stopped before and don't know what to expect.

D. It could be *apathy* if you really don't care.

E. It could be *contempt* if this is the tenth time you have been stopped and you feel you are being harrassed.

F. It could be *total surprise* if you know you have done nothing wrong (but what you don't know is, your taillight *is* out).

VS. THE POLICEMAN'S FRAME OF MIND

Before we discuss what to do, let's examine the policeman's state of mind. He could be brand new, three months on the job and may be quite unsure of himself and inexperienced in enforcing traffic laws. He could have twenty years on the job and figures he has heard every excuse, lie and rationalization there is and has hardened himself

15

against those things. His personality could be quite lenient or even very strict, depending somewhat on his background. Also, the officer may have just been verbally reprimanded by the sergeant because the quality or quantity of his work is not up to the standard or performance established by his peers. It is also quite possible that he may have just been awarded the title "Officer Of The Year" for services rendered to the community. What if his wife just walked out on him this morning and told him she is taking him for everything he has?

Regardless of what the officer's frame of mind is—or what yours is—it all boils down to one thing: He has made an observation that caused him to believe that something about your driving or your car is not legal and that you should get a ticket because of it.

You will notice that I have said quite a bit about attitudes and frames of mind. Why is that? Because you are human and the officer is human and *everything one does is directly related to his or her attitude at the time.*

THE BOTTOM LINE

So this is it. This is the bottom line. Pay close attention. **If there is a way to 'talk your way out' of a ticket, it is going to depend almost totally on YOUR attitude.**

Does it matter what the policeman's attitude is? In terms of helping you avoid getting a ticket ... **NO. It makes little or no difference.**

16

The responsibility for maintaining a good attitude is going to fall back on you. For example, if the officer confronts you with an overbearing, sarcastic attitude, are you willing to put up with it? If not—if you feel you just have to tell the cop what you think—then be prepared to receive the ticket. It's almost guaranteed. But, if you are willing to use the common sense information provided here to your best advantage and use it intelligently, then it's possible I can help you avoid getting a ticket. There are no guarantees, however. Who is to anticipate, for instance, the cop who is nearing the end of his shift on the last day of the month and only needs one more ticket to bring his performance up from last month when he got chewed out ... and unfortunately you just made a rolling stop through a stop sign?

[NOTE: If the above statement sounded as though I am referring to a "quota", it was not intended that way. I don't know if any police departments in the U.S. have quota systems to establish standards of performance. In California, and many other states I have checked with, it is illegal for law enforcement agencies to impose a quota on their officers. But let's face it—you hired us to 'get' the turkey who just cut you off or who just totalled out your brand-new Porsche and now you would like him or her to receive a nice traffic ticket and/or a punch in the mouth if possible. So, how many tickets do you want us to write? You, as a taxpayer, want us to protect you from other drivers who may not have your well-being in mind. It has been proven that tickets are a deterrent to those who would intentionally violate the law. So ... how many?

17

We can't come up with a specific number, remember? No quota. I think you probably just want us to go out and catch and ticket the worst ones. Those violations that are not so bad, you probably just want us to bring them to the drivers' attention and give him or her a warning so it won't happen again, right? I think that's a reasonable request. My boss thinks so too and all he asks is that I go out and do a good job and try not to let my job performance fall too far below the average performance of other officers who are working the same beat at the same time of day. I consider myself an objective person and I really can't come up with anything more reasonable than that. If I'm not capable of enforcing the law, I should probably look for a different type of work.

There are no quotas! There is only an expectation that a reasonable level of performance is achieved based on traffic flow conditions, the accident statistics at any given location, the time of day, weather conditions, the average level of performance established by other officers having the same duties, etc.]

* * *

To summarize what I mean about the importance of *your* attitude: **you need to create an attitude in your mind and through your words and actions that conveys to the officer a willingness on your part to comply with the law. This attitude needs to be presented with a SPIRIT OF COOPERATION.**

As you read on through this book you will find more specific examples of attitudes and their probable effects on the outcomes of police/violator confrontations.

❊❊❊❊❊❊❊❊❊❊❊❊❊❊❊❊❊❊❊❊❊❊❊❊❊❊❊❊❊❊

After stopping an attorney for "tailgating" (within one car-length) at 65 mph on the freeway, he gave me this one: "Give me a break, Officer! You have to follow other cars closely on the freeway. If you allow too much space, other cars squeeze in and you keep losing ground!" (Yes, he got a ticket.)

❊❊❊❊❊❊❊❊❊❊❊❊❊❊❊❊❊❊❊❊❊❊❊❊❊❊❊❊❊❊

LEMME SEE YER LICENSE!

DOs & DON'Ts

You may instantly like the policeman who stops you. He may be warm, friendly, intelligent and professional. Or, you could be wondering how this stark, raving maniac with the IQ of a plant could have been hired in the first place. *Guess what? It doesn't matter! Be cool.*

It is important to keep your composure and be friendly and polite **without appearing as though you are trying to 'butter' him up.** Try to maintain an attitude that conveys this to the officer: **I'm not sure if I know exactly what I've done wrong. But I know you had a good reason for stopping me. So I'm at your mercy. But, are you willing to discuss the situation for a moment?**

Besides your attitude and what you say, your **actions** can also make a big difference.

DO's:

1. ***Pull over as soon as possible*** when you see the officer's red lights behind you. In most instances, the officer will have already picked out the safest place for you both to stop prior to turning on his lights. Even if he hasn't, you don't want to make him mad, do you? So *pull over!* Besides, ignoring his lights won't make him go away—as surprising as that may seem to some people. ***Always keep in mind that cooperation is essential!***

2. ***Roll your window down*** so the officer doesn't have to knock to get your attention. ***If your radio is on—turn it off.***

3. ***Keep your registration, proof-of-insurance card and drivers license where they are easily accessible*** (e.g. overhead visor or in an *uncluttered* glove compartment). You'd be surprised how many motorists end up searching their car from top to bottom—including the trunk— for these.

4. ***Stay in your car*** unless the officer asks you to step outside. Some people feel it is a sign of courtesy or friendliness to quickly exit their vehicle and greet the officer. However, most officers prefer that you remain seated in your vehicle until the approach is made. It will be safer for you to do so because of passing traffic— plus, it gives the officer more time to size-up the situation and pre-determine any existing hazards prior to making the

approach. *[NOTE: Besides, if a person is in a hurry to get out and meet me, I begin to suspect that he or she doesn't want me to proceed up to their vehicle where I can look inside and find an open container of alcohol or some other incriminating evidence. If I suspect this is the case, I will look over the vehicle interior thoroughly.]*

5. ***Keep your hands where the officer can see them—at all times!*** He hopes you don't have a gun, knife or flame-thrower and it makes him nervous if he can't see what you're doing with your hands.

6. ***Be as cool, calm and collected as you can.*** And ***be polite*** regardless of any negative thoughts you may be having. Even if his first words are, "Well now, that was kind of stupid, wasn't it? Lemme see your license!" Just say, "Yes, Officer" (or say *nothing)* and hand him your driver's license.

7. ***Politely, inquire why you were stopped*** (if you *truly* don't know). You might start out by saying, "Have I done something wrong, Officer?" But, if your violation was so obvious that a five-year-old child would have recognized it, **don't ask**, because the cop will know that you know exactly what you did. If this is the case, you might say something like, "I'm sorry, I didn't see that other car until it was too late." Or, "I'm sorry, I didn't realize I was going that fast until I saw your red lights. I guess my mind was on where I was going. Will you excuse me this time?"

* * *

In most cases, it is better to ask an innocent question than to make a specific statement. The following questions are not all inclusive and will not cover every situation. Common sense should be your guide in whether or not to use any of these in your case. You may feel more comfortable with your own wording that conveys the same attitude:

A. "How can I fix my car so it will be totally legal, Officer?"

B. "I am normally a very safe driver, Officer, but for a second my attention was elsewhere. I promise I will try to be more careful."

C. "Insurance for a person my age is quite high, so I have been trying to keep my record clean. Could you trust me to not make the same mistake again?"

D. "I don't understand the violation you said I made. Will you please explain it to me, Officer?"

E. "I have a perfect driving record. If you just give me a warning this time, I'll do my best to keep it that way."

F. "I didn't realize that was illegal. I wouldn't have done it if I had known. I certainly know now!"

G. "I know this situation is my own fault. Can you excuse me this time? I promise you won't have to stop me again."

H. "It has been a long drive. You just made me realize I need to stop and get some coffee."

I. "I'm new to this area, Officer. I guess I need to pay closer attention to my driving."

J. "I know I was going a little fast, but I have an *emergency*. I'm taking my son (daughter, wife, neighbor, friend) to the hospital for treatment!" *[NOTE: **Don't lie** about this. The officer may take your license and follow you to the hospital to see if you do have a **real** emergency]*

K. "I'm sorry, I should be paying closer attention. My boyfriend just broke up with me and it's hard to concentrate on other things right now. But I promise I'll be more careful."

L. "Officer, is there something I can do or say that you will make a decision not to write a ticket this time and give me just a warning instead?"

SERIOUS VIOLATIONS

If you have done something of a serious nature, and you know it, you may realize there is no way out of any enforcement action a policeman might take. If that is the case, it may be better for you not to discuss your violation at all. Be cooperative, but let the policeman do all the talking. You may want to call an attorney later, before saying something to the officer that might incriminate you.

For instance, if you just burned your rear tires for 250 feet and lost control, sliding sideways into a mailbox, narrowly missing two elderly pedestrians—and you did all this right in front of a policeman—what can you say? The answer obviously is, "When do I appear in court, Officer?"

LYING AND ITS CONSEQUENCES

Unfortunately, I cannot tell you *exactly* what to say. Each person and each situation will be different. Above all, know this: **if you lie, rationalize, become sarcastic or in any way insinuate that the officer is lying, you will probably get the ticket**.

And let me re-emphasize: you don't want to make any statements that may be used against you later in court. For example, if the officer says you were going 70 miles an hour in a 55 zone, it is better to say, "I'm sorry, I didn't realize I was going that fast" than to say, "I was watching my speedometer and I never went over 62!" You have just admitted to driving 7 miles per hour over the 55 MPH speed limit! **In most cases, the less said by you the better off you will be**.

* * *

Next are some things **not** to do or say. Once again, in the case of quoted lines of speech, these are not specific, as personalities and situations differ. I have attempted to instill a general "attitude" to avoid.

DON'Ts:

1. When you have been signalled to stop, while traveling on a freeway, **don't pull into the center divider section**—unless you want to make a stark-raving maniac out of the otherwise professional officer behind you. In parking near the center divider, even though it is not a normal traffic lane, you could well be the cause of a bad wreck or mishap! If you're not on a freeway, just try to remember to attempt to get as far removed from the traffic flow as possible, wherever the officer stops you. That way he doesn't have to worry about you or him being struck by a passing car.

2. **Don't hand the officer your wallet.** He doesn't want to be accused of stealing your money, so he will not accept the whole wallet. He will wait until *you* remove the license.

3. **Never say, "You can't write me a ticket—I haven't done anything wrong!"** The officer will take this as a challenge and will be *sure* to write you a ticket. He can then let the judge determine whether or not you have done anything wrong.

4. ***Never say, "I have had five tickets. If you write me one more I'll lose my license!"*** The officer will most likely feel that if your driving is that bad, he *should* write you the ticket. It may get you off the road for awhile and make it safer for others.

5. ***Don't cry*** (especially if you are a man!), it rarely works. Most officers feel that a female who cries over a traffic stop is trying to gain the policeman's sympathy and he will refuse to be influenced or intimidated by the performance. Some women are very emotional and will begin to cry uncontrollably. But whether the crying is for real or just an act, it just doesn't help the situation.

6. ***Don't tell an officer you will take the matter to court***—whether or not you are planning to go to court and fight the ticket. If you tell him during the stop, he will be better prepared to beat you in court by taking meticulous notes concerning your violation. If he thinks you have graciously accepted the ticket, he may not make any notes at all. If your case comes up three months from the time the ticket was issued, his memory may not be that good. In addition, telling the officer you will go to court will be taken as a challenge and a further incentive to go ahead and write the ticket.

7. **Don't beg to be let off.** Begging is not an admirable human characteristic and will probably cause the officer to *want* to write you a ticket.

8. **Never threaten.** For example, I have had people threaten to 'see me in court'; threaten to 'get' my wife and kids; 'get' me later off-duty; or threaten not to appear in court. None of these worked. All they do is make a person who might be relatively lenient suddenly become very strict about enforcing *all* the laws you have violated—including criminal charges that may result from your threats.

9. **Don't refuse to sign the ticket.** Sign it even if you feel that the officer has made a mistake. Your signature is only a promise to appear in court to clear up the matter and is not an admission of any guilt on your part. You can always tell the court later that you feel the officer made an honest mistake, and why. If you refuse to sign the ticket you can be arrested and taken to jail.

10. **Don't argue about the violation.** It is okay to tell your side of the story and why you did what you did—or that you feel you didn't actually violate the law and why. Arguing will only put the officer on the defensive and make him feel even more justified about writing you a ticket.

11. **Don't try to get out of a ticket by using titles or name-dropping.** It normally won't work. In fact, with some officers it may achieve the opposite effect that you desire. Some titles include: Senator, Mayor, Councilman, Chief, Captain, Doctor, Lawyer, Editor or Publisher, Priest, Rabbi or Minister. If you are one of these or are close friends with one, you usually will not influence the officer by letting him or her know. On the other hand, where there are people, there are politics. You show me a job with no politics and I'll show you a group of robots. While name-dropping has worked on some occasions, my advice is not to try it. Should you decide to do so, you are on your own.

[NOTE: If you DO get ticketed, DON'T FAIL TO CLEAR UP THE TICKET THROUGH THE COURT—either by mail or in person, whichever is required in your case. Failing to do so will only result in a warrant being issued for your arrest. Besides, the same cop who wrote you the ticket may be the one who gets to lock you up—you wouldn't want that to happen, would you?]

* * *

What I hope I have conveyed to you is to *do and say things that will cause the officer to like and trust you*. What you will be doing, psychologically, is making it difficult for one human being to punish another human being. If the situation progresses in a positive manner from the time the officer turns the red lights on, it will become increasingly difficult for him or her to be mindful of the importance of why you were stopped in the first place. It's kind of like a parent/child relationship. If a child spills milk all over the kitchen table, you may feel like swatting her across the behind. But, what if the child smiles up at you and says, "Gosh Mom, I know I spilled my milk again, but it was just an accident. I really have been trying not to do it anymore. Please forgive me?" *Now* punish her—if you can.

✽✽✽✽✽✽✽✽✽✽✽✽✽✽✽✽✽✽✽✽✽✽✽✽✽✽✽✽✽✽✽

The driver asked, "Don't you work with Officer Smith? He's a good friend of mine. I've known him a long time!" (name dropping) Regardless, I gave him a ticket. Later, out of curiosity, I asked that particular officer if he knew my "violator". Officer Smith said, "Yeah, I know the jerk. He drives like a maniac! Last time I stopped him, he wanted my badge number and threatened to report me to his 'friend', the captain."

✽✽✽✽✽✽✽✽✽✽✽✽✽✽✽✽✽✽✽✽✽✽✽✽✽✽✽✽✽✽✽

I WAS SPEEDING SO I COULD MAKE IT TO A GAS
STATION AND MY CIGARETTES DROPPED ON THE
FLOOR SO I MISSED THE LIGHT AND MY
ACCELERATOR GOT STUCK AND MY DRIVER'S
LICENSE IS IN MY OTHER PANTS AND...

COP - OUTS

Let's face it— we don't like to be wrong. Even if you know you are wrong, you don't want anyone else to know it. There are those who will admit when they have made a mistake and those who will *never* admit to one.

If a cop stops you, guess what? He's going to tell you—***you are wrong!*** Have you ever heard of a cop stopping someone and saying, "Sir, that was really an excellent right hand turn you made back there and I just wanted to compliment you on it!"? Or, "Wow, that's the first time I've ever seen anyone stop right at the limit line. Your bumper was within two inches of it. I am really impressed!" It's not going to happen!

The officer is going to try to cast a shadow of doubt on your ability to operate a motor vehicle. Furthermore, he will probably accuse you of *intentionally* violating a traffic law (even though, in most cases, *intent* is not a necessary element for a ticket). And, in some cases, you may be accused of violating an obscure law you've never even heard of.

EXCUSES, EXCUSES, EXCUSES

Some folks are so set against being told they are wrong, they will rationalize or fabricate a total lie. They will even plead not guilty in court for no other reason than to show someone else they are not wrong and to try to prove that the policeman was wrong—especially if they didn't like his personality!

There are some people who will tell the truth ("Yes, Officer, you're right, I'm a little late and I was going 65."). Most people will rationalize ("I may not have made a full stop at the stop sign, but I could see no one was coming, so it was okay." And some people will flat-out lie ("My license? Uh... I must have left it in my other pants!"—a computer check shows the license was revoked a year ago.)

Police Officers hear a wide variety of 'excuses' over the years. The following are a few of the most common excuses (which, for the record, almost *never* work):

1. "I'm almost out of gas. I was speeding so I could make it to a gas station!"

2. "I had to hurry! My little girl has to go to the bathroom!"

3. "My cigarettes dropped on the floor and when I picked them up I must have missed the stop sign."

4. "I don't know where that open bottle of whiskey came from. My wife must have left it in here."

5. "My driver's license is home on the dresser." (More than likely it has actually been suspended by the state!)

[NOTE: If you are stopped and you really did leave your driver's license at home, you will be asked for some other form of ID—such as a registration card, social security card, fishing license, or anything "official" with your name on it. The very least that will happen to you without a license is you will receive a ticket requiring you to furnish proof of a valid license to the court. This may or may not involve a fine. However, if the officer is not convinced you are who you say you are, he may take you to jail until you are able to prove your identity. Use your imagination to ascertain how long that might take.]

6. "I have to drive fast! I have an *emergency!* My mother-in-law is sick with the flu and requires my wife's immediate attention!"

7. "I wasn't speeding intentionally. My carburetor gets stuck wide open once in a while." (And millions of other similar excuses where the driver blames the car for his or her mistakes.)

8. "I know my registration expired last year, but I am just on my way now to the DMV to take care of it!"

9. "I didn't know it was against the law to park in a red zone here. There are no signs!"

10. "I would have stopped at the stop sign but my brakes went out ... gee, that's funny, they seem to be okay now!"

11. "Honesht Oshifer, I only had two beersh ... hic!"

The list goes on and on. Once in a while a brand new one will slip in, but most are easily recognizable as *cop-outs* by experienced officers.

* * *

The following are actual quotes taken from accident report forms over the years. They are humorous in that they show a tendency people have to excuse their own actions by trying to affix blame on something or someone else:

"The telephone pole was approaching fast. I was attempting to swerve out of its path when it struck my front end."

"My car was legally parked as it backed into the other vehicle."

"I was sure that the old fellow would never make it to the other side of the road when I struck him."

"I don't know what happened because I was thrown from my car as it left the road. I was later found in a ditch by some stray cows."

"Coming home I drove into the wrong driveway and collided with a tree I don't have."

"I thought my window was down but found out it was up when I put my head through it."

"The pedestrian hit me and went under my car."

"In my attempt to kill a fly, I drove into a telephone pole."

"I was on my way to the doctor's with rear end trouble when my universal joint gave way causing me to have an accident."

"The pedestrian had no idea what direction to go, so I ran over him."

"As I approached the intersection, a stop sign suddenly appeared in a place where no stop sign had ever appeared before and I was unable to stop in time."

"The other car collided with mine without giving any warning of its intentions."

"The truck carelessly backed through my windshield into my wife's face."

"The guy was all over the road. I had to swerve a number of times before I hit him."

"I had been shopping for plants all day and was on my way home. As I reached an intersection, a hedge sprang up obscuring my vision. I did not see the other car."

"To avoid hitting the bumper of the car in front, I struck the pedestrian."

"An invisible car came out of nowhere, struck my vehicle, and vanished."

"The indirect cause of this accident was a little guy in a small car with a big mouth."

* * *

The purpose of this chapter has been to make you aware that if you are going to try to talk your way out of a ticket, you might want to think twice about making up an excuse for your actions. As I stated before, most excuses are quite transparent—there are only a few that may be considered valid in the officer's mind. If you have a real emergency like an injury or life threatening situation, the officer should not ticket you.

Once I stopped a young man for failing to stop for a stop sign. He told me he was the manager of a local restaurant, that someone had broken in during the night, stolen some money and that he was on his way to assess the situation. He said he felt he had an emergency. The few seconds or a minute he was trying to save would not have mattered at this point (his money and the thieves who took it were already long gone). I told him I did not consider his situation an emergency and he was ticketed. It has to be a *real* emergency.

A tree that has grown and partially obscured a stop sign *may* be considered a valid excuse by an officer. A malfunctioning traffic signal could be an excuse. The officer will probably want to check the signal for himself, however.

WHEN TO CALL IT QUITS

There is a point at which it is too late to "talk your way out of a traffic ticket" (with the possible exception being if you have a life-threatening emergency or something nearly as severe). Specifically, that point in time is when the officer's pen touches paper. Once the ticket writing has begun, it takes virtually an "Act of Congress" to reverse the procedure. Each traffic ticket is numbered and every officer is accountable for the numbers issued to him. In order to void a traffic ticket an officer is required to justify, in writing, the reason for doing so. This justification must be approved by his supervisors and it is almost never done. (The justification would be an obvious mistake or error in judgement which came to the officer's attention later on.)

This doesn't mean your vocal cords need to be severed at the very instant pen touches paper, but the point is, once started, the ticket will most likely be finished. Talking about the violation at this point is pretty much a waste of your breath.

MUST THE OFFICER GIVE YOU A CHANCE TO "TALK YOUR WAY..."?

There is no specific rule or procedure which mandates that a police officer *must* listen to your story or excuse before he writes you a ticket. His or her mind may already be made up based on what was observed. *Theoretically, your guilt or innocence is to be determined by the court.* However, as mentioned throughout this book, human relations (the officer-violator contact) will play a major role.

It is merely common courtesy and professionalism on the part of the officer which dictates that he or she should at least listen to your explanation or version of the incident before making a decision to write the ticket or let you off with a verbal warning.

Should you encounter an uncaring or incompassionate officer who just isn't interested in listening, then you may want to consider other options outlined later in this book.

* * *

In summary, if you are going to use an excuse to try to explain an obvious violation, it had better be *real good* and it had better be *the truth* or you can count on getting a ticket.

❀❀❀❀❀❀❀❀❀❀❀❀❀❀❀❀❀❀❀❀❀❀❀❀❀❀❀

After being stopped for speeding, this driver stated, "Officer, am I glad I found you! I saw a car going really fast and I was just trying to catch up with it so I could get a license number and turn it over to the police. Didn't you see him?" (Ticket!)

❀❀❀❀❀❀❀❀❀❀❀❀❀❀❀❀❀❀❀❀❀❀❀❀❀❀❀

EXPERIENCES

To help you understand why and how a policeman reacts as he does, I am going to relate to you a few experiences and reactions of my own.

I have seen what appeared to me at the time to be deliberate violations of the law (running a stop sign or red light, making an unsafe lane change, tailgating at 65 mph., etc.) and made up my mind that "that driver is going to get a ticket!" I would pull him over, walk up to his car with my ticket book and find that this is really a nice guy. He failed to stop for the stop sign because he is new to the area and he's a little late for the first day on a new job as a clerk in a department store. There, he will probably earn barely enough to feed and support his four very polite children sitting in the back seat of his aging station wagon (He had to drop them off at his mother's before work.). His wife is presently in the hospital recovering from complications developed when she had her last child. That child is now six months old! I said to myself, "Boy, this poor guy has enough problems without me writing him a ticket. That's all he needs now is to have to pay a $50 fine on top of everything else and maybe to lose a day off work at his new job. I just can't do it." I would then tell him not to be so careless in the future and let him go with just a warning.

On the other hand, I have seen similar violations, maybe not quite so serious in nature where I had to decide whether or not it was even worth it to pull the guy over. In one instance I hadn't been very busy—the day had been a little boring and I thought I might establish some good public relations by stopping this guy and just giving him a polite verbal warning. So I pulled him over and the conversation went something like this:

OFFICER KELLEY
Good morning.

VIOLATOR
(sneering)
What's your problem, cop?

OFFICER KELLEY
(pause—regaining composure)
Sir, I stopped you for driving five miles-per-hour over the maximum speed limit.

VIOLATOR
Oh bullcrap! I saw you back there. You never got a clock on me and I know I never went over 55!

OFFICER KELLEY
May I see your driver's license, please?

VIOLATOR
Yeah, right on. You know, you guys oughta be out catching real criminals instead of pickin' on somebody you think went two miles over the speed limit. Are you gonna make your quota for today?

OFFICER KELLEY
Do you still live at the same address, Sir?

VIOLATOR
Well, I really don't think it's any of your
business, but yes I do.

OFFICER KELLEY
That's fine, Sir. Well, you know the speed
limit *is* 55 and you were going 60, so I'm
going to have to write you a ticket. I'll be
right back.

Get the picture?

I'm not implying that whether you get a ticket
or not depends *solely* on your attitude. A professional police officer is quite aware that he is also
dealing with a wide variety of human beings with
all sorts of human reactions. And, he is realistic
enough to know that enforcement of the laws
needs to be based on the principles and reasons
the rules were enacted in the first place.

Many departments teach their officers in the
beginning not to enforce laws according to the
attitudes and reactions of the people with whom
they come in contact. They teach them to be firm,
yet fair, impartial, unbiased and not to prejudge
anyone. But you and I both know that people are
people and it doesn't always happen that way.

* * *

CASE HISTORIES

This excuse crops up periodically: I stopped a truck tractor and flatbed trailer for doing 80 mph in a 55 mph zone. The driver looked at me earnestly and said, "I just drove up here from L.A. [500 miles away] and I've had a problem with my throttle sticking open. I'm going to fix it when I get back home." (He got a ticket.)

* * *

A man was driving along a freeway in the Los Angeles area. His wife and three-year-old son were passengers. The boy was standing in the middle of the front seat. The man had passed his freeway exit and was becoming frustrated and annoyed because he was now lost. A little voice said, "Daddy, I have to go potty." Daddy said, "Not now, I'm busy." A minute later, "Daddy, I have to go potty real bad." Daddy replied angrily, "Go find a pocket to pee in and don't bother me!" Daddy was deeply engrossed in trying to find his destination in L.A. traffic when he was startled by something that felt very warm and wet on the right side of his body—which caused him to jerk the wheel and swerve across a traffic lane. The swerving happened with a Highway Patrol car behind him. It turned out that the boy had innocently obeyed his father but the only pocket he could find was in Daddy's suit jacket which Daddy was still wearing. This story was related to the patrolman. Physical evidence was also presented. (The patrolman had a good laugh and Daddy didn't get a ticket.)

* * *

48

A big-rig truck driver, after being stopped for doing 75 mph, said, "Officer, I have been married for 15 years. When I come home from work at night, it seems my wife is never in the mood—if you know what I mean. I have been on the road for six days now and I just phoned her to let her know I'll be home in an hour. She told me she is *in the mood*. I am hurrying to get home before she changes her mind!" (According to my source, he did not get a ticket.) I guess there's no use trying to slow a good man down!

YOU'RE NOT TAGGING ME BECAUSE I WAS
SPEEDING—YOU'RE JUST PREJUDICED
AGAINST MARTIANS!

POLICE PREJUDICE

Are you more likely to receive a ticket if you are driving a souped-up car? How about if you are a teenager? Are the police really more likely to 'pick on you' because you are black or brown or red or yellow? If I said no, I would be contradicting the theme of this book which constantly refers to the interactions of human beings. If I said yes, it would not be totally true either. Therefore, I will have to say, "sometimes".

Are there *some* policemen who dislike teen-agers? or hot rods? or sports cars? or different races of people? or different nationalities?

Are there *some* teenagers who dislike the police for no other reason than they represent authority? Are there different races of people who dislike the police just because they believe that *all* police are prejudiced? Are there groups of people, like motor-cycle gangs, who dislike the police because they believe cops will *never* treat them fairly?

Obviously, there are no simple answers.

In my personal experience, the percentage of police who have some of the previously listed prejudices is small. Also, their numbers are diminishing with passing time as more and more people are becoming aware of the feelings of minorities and the importance of human rights and equality. I personally believe strongly in these rights.

A MESSAGE TO TEENAGERS AND YOUNG DRIVERS

You represent a unique problem to the police. You are youthfully spirited, energetic, enthusiastic and impulsive. You have experienced few of the responsibilities associated with surviving in a complex society and you sometimes have the feeling that you are somehow invincible! I know how you feel—I've been there. Sometimes your relatively carefree attitudes are reflected and transmitted out of your bodies, into the steering wheel and accelerator and out of the tires, finding little or no resistance against the pavement. I'm speaking in generalities, of course, as obviously not all of you are hot-rodders. Even though some of you do create problems at times, I find it hard to be too critical because, after all, you are one of us. I believe you can benefit tremendously from the information in this book because we are talking mostly about attitudes. When a policeman stops a teenager who is driving a high performance car, already there is one strike against him. If the teenager has a chip on his shoulder and his attitude reflects it, he will have *three* strikes against him.

SPORTS CARS = MORE TICKETS?

Sports cars, hot rods, high performance cars, specialty cars, motorcycles, Corvettes / Ferraris / Lamborghinis or any vehicle that is extraordinary *will* attract the attention of the police. I find myself watching a Corvette a little more closely on the freeway than other cars. Why? Obviously, the car was designed for speed and handling. That makes it a more likely candidate for a speeding ticket (And that's part of my job—to write speeding tickets, right?).

People driving these kinds of vehicles are more likely to be stopped by the police for minor violations than those driving standard automobiles—if, for no other reason, simply because they draw attention to themselves. (Ironically, this is often why the driver bought one of these special vehicles in the first place—to attract attention. Well, it worked—they do attract attention—especially the policeman's.) Even so, there will still be human contact between the driver and the cop—which is where this book comes in.

WHAT IF YOU DO EXPERIENCE PREJUDICE?

Preconceived ideas in the minds of the police about young people, extraordinary vehicles, different races or nationalities or any other form of prejudice exists to some degree. What can you do about it if you find that you seem to fit into one of these categories?

If you are a teenager, or a sports car driver, or if your skin color is not the same as the cop, **never say,** "The only reason you stopped me is... because I'm a kid", or "because I drive a Porsche", or "because I'm Oriental", or "because of my long hair and beard", or "because I'm from out of state." If you insinuate that the officer is prejudiced, it will not cause him to prove that he isn't by letting you go. It will cause him to write the ticket because you have just accused him of not living up to the image of having a high standard of fairness and impartiality that is expected of him. He will not like you for having brought those charges against him whether or not he does, in fact, have certain prejudices.

My advice is stick to the common sense principles outlined in this book, which will give you the best chance to avoid that ticket!

* * *

To summarize my personal feelings on the issue of police prejudice, I would like to make the following statements:

I am a graduate of both the Pomona California Police Academy and the California Highway Patrol Academy. I have an Associate of Arts Degree in Administration of Justice with specialization in the subjects of self-image psychology and success motivation principles. In over twenty-six years of law enforcement experience, I have had friends and acquaintances who are police officers, deputy sheriffs, narcotic agents, fish and game wardens, FBI agents, deputy district attorneys, lawyers, judges, probation officers and many others involved directly or indirectly with our judicial system. We are all individuals and need to be recognized as such. People do not like to be labeled or categorized. Black people do not. Yellow people do not. Brown, Red and White people do not. And policemen/women do not.

In my years of experience in dealing with all kinds of people, on both sides of the law, I have reached a few conclusions: There are good and bad doctors. There are good and bad lawyers. There are also good and bad policemen/police-women. Fortunately for all of us, the bad ones in any profession or occupation are in a very small minority. We only ask that you judge us as individuals and not to let a negative news article or a negative experience with one bad policeman influence you to believe that you are not well protected. Even though it may sometimes seem as if that were not true, *most* of the law enforcement people I have known have your best interests in mind. Most of them want to do a good job of enforcing traffic laws and all laws for that matter. This way, not only will you and your family be safe, but theirs will too.

SMILE — YOU'RE ON CANDID RADAR!

RADAR

What are your chances of talking your way out of a radar ticket? Slim or none? Remember: it is still the human being that writes the ticket and not the radar unit! In fact, you can reverse that state of affairs in your favor if you intend to defend a radar ticket in court. Your best defense will probably be to challenge the ability of the operator (officer) of the device rather than the accuracy of the unit itself.

In order to "beat" a radar ticket in court, you are going to have to do more research than normal prior to your trial. There are a variety of different radar devices presently in use by the police. Some are hand-held and others are mounted in or on the police vehicle. There are different makes and models of radar units just as there are different CB radios, each with differing features. You need to know which type is being used in your area.

HOW RADAR WORKS

The radar unit itself, in determining the speed of a moving *object*, is very accurate. The technical theory behind its use is called the Doppler Effect. But most radars can be "fooled" by certain objects and may be "clocking" the wrong vehicle. For instance, if two vehicles are in close proximity and both are going in the same direction, but one is a large truck and the other a car, the radar will probably pick out the large vehicle. Some radar units have been "confused" by aluminum foil which was stuffed into the nose of a vehicle by its owner. However, it is my understanding that this procedure is not effective against many of the newer radar units and is therefore not recommended. Also, radar is not as effective in picking out fiberglass vehicles like Corvettes, Excalibers, replicars, etc. Like any other mechanical or electrical device, radar is also subject to malfunction or failure.

The accuracy of the radar unit may be affected by changes in temperature or outside interference by an electrical source. For these reasons, the operator is required to make sure the unit is calibrated periodically and that it is functioning properly. It is the responsibility of the operator to make sure that the unit is "clocking" the correct vehicle. He may be asked in court to furnish proof that the unit was calibrated and in good working order on the day the ticket was written. He will have to testify as to how many other vehicles were on the road at the time and how far they were from the ticketed vehicle. He may be asked to show that the unit was pointed and set right.

[NOTE: In some states (e.g. California), radar may not be used as evidence on some streets and highways if a "speed survey" was not obtained and recorded by the Department of Transportation prior to its use. (Make inquiries about this when you prepare for court.)]

Many officers have a tendency to work close to their "targets" to eliminate the possibility of error. Also, by being close, they can quickly make a U-turn to make the stop. If you are paying attention to your driving, you may even spot the police vehicle prior to being picked up on radar.

As you can see, radar is not infallible. But it *is* very accurate and not that easy to beat in court. It is an excellent tool for the police because of its accuracy and because of the psychological effect. Most drivers, if they know radar is being used in an area, will automatically slow down. Therefore the desired effect is being achieved by the police even if there are no radar units on the road on a particular day.

RADAR DETECTOR— GOOD OR BAD IDEA?

Since we are on the subject of radar, you may be wondering about the feasibility of purchasing a radar detector. These devices are readily available for purchase in many electronic outlets or through automotive magazine advertisements by mail-order. Their purpose is, of course, to alert you to the use of radar in a given area by detecting the electrical impulses given off by police radar units. A good radar detector can sometimes pick up these impulses from up to three times farther than the radar unit itself is effective at determining a vehicle's speed. In most instances, this allows enough time to slow down prior to being "clocked" by the police radar.

The disadvantages of radar detectors are, first of all, they are illegal in several states not only to use, but to possess. In some cases they have been seized and held as evidence by the police. Check the laws in your own state to determine the legality of a radar detector. Secondly, they are almost totally ineffective against the type of police radar referred to as "instant-on" radar. This type of radar unit does not send out or emit a constant signal as do many of the other types. It can be switched on to instantly determine the speed of an oncoming vehicle without having to go through a warm up phase. By the time a radar detector picks up a signal from one of these units it is too late to slow down. You are had! And lastly, there are a few political groups attempting to outlaw the manufacture and sale of radar detectors—the theory being that the only purpose of a radar detector is to break the law.

* * *

In summary, the only sure-fire way to "beat" a radar ticket is to stay within the speed limit.

❈❈❈❈❈❈❈❈❈❈❈❈❈❈❈❈❈❈❈❈❈❈❈❈❈❈❈❈❈❈

Some people will go to any lengths to get out of a ticket: After writing a speeding ticket, the patrolman returned to the driver's window to have him sign it. He found the driver to be deceased. The driver could not be revived and was later determined to have had a heart attack. Luckily, this does not happen very often.

❈❈❈❈❈❈❈❈❈❈❈❈❈❈❈❈❈❈❈❈❈❈❈❈❈❈❈❈❈❈

DRUNK DRIVING

For many people, drinking is fun. But driving while under the influence of alcohol is not funny.

Every year in the United States somewhere around 50,000 to 55,000 men, women and children are *killed* on our highways. **Fifty percent** or more of these deaths are caused by drivers who have been drinking.

Let me clear up one common misconception. "Drunk Driving" is inaccurate terminology. You do not have to be drunk to be a menace on the highway or even to be arrested. You only have to be influenced to some degree by the alcohol you have consumed. One drink or one beer will influence you to some degree (depending on numerous factors such as tolerance, body weight, metabolism, etc.) and the more alcohol consumed, the greater the influence. "Influence" in this sense means your mental attitude will change and important things, like driving carefully, may no longer matter to you. *(NOTE: I do not wish to insinuate that **all** drinking drivers are wantonly careless. Some are trying to drive carefully, but their mental alertness and reflexes are "handicapped" by the alcohol.)* Additionally, it will take you more time to react as your alcohol consumption increases.

SHOULD YOU FEEL SAFE IF YOU'VE ONLY HAD ONE BEER?

Often, the person who has had *"only two or three beers"* is more dangerous behind the wheel than the one who is obviously "drunk"—because the drunk knows he is drunk and knows he has to use some caution or he won't make it home. The person who has had "only two or three drinks" usually thinks he or she is still fully capable of driving—then causes others to suffer for this careless and foolish mistake.

We have a saying that makes this point: "High Speed, Low B.A." Translated, this means that if a driver has been drinking and is driving at a high rate of speed, chances are his blood-alcohol content will be low. Low could mean anywhere from .03% to .10%. In California, the law presumes that everyone who tests at a .10% blood alcohol content or above is under the influence of alcohol. The point is that even if you have only consumed enough drinks to bring your B.A. content up to a .05%, you will *usually* be under the influence enough at that level to cause you to drive too fast for safety.

SAFETY TIPS

I have said some relatively serious things here, but I am realistic enough to know that, armed with this information, most people who enjoy drinking will continue to drive after drinking anyway. Sad, but true. So I am offering the following information to those of you who are responsible enough to know the legal limits set forth by your own state laws. And to those who know when you are affected enough by your drinking that you should not get behind the wheel of a motor vehicle under any circumstances.

Nothing in this information should be construed to be a guarantee of freedom from arrest or an endorsement to drink and drive!

If you have made the wrong decision and choose to continue to drink and drive, what is the best way to 1. Avoid getting killed? 2. Avoid killing someone else? 3. Stay out of jail?

You are behind the wheel and you have recently had a couple drinks or more and are influenced some (feeling a slight "buzz") by the alcohol (or you may be totally unaware of it). Here are some things that should help:

1. Roll down a window or two and don't turn on the heater—this way it will be easier for you to stay awake.

2. Drive in as straight a line as you possibly can. Keep your vehicle entirely within your own lane.

3. Do not drive much slower or much faster than the posted speed limit. This way it's safer for you and everyone else around you.

4. Concentrate harder on stop signs and red lights. Your reactions are slower than you think.

5. Don't play soft music on the radio. Very likely, it will lull you to sleep.

6. If you do start to feel drowsy, stop and get some coffee and stretch your legs. Or, pull over to a safe place off the road and sleep for a while. Getting home late or being uncomfortable for a couple hours is better than the alternative of falling asleep at the wheel.

7. In general, you should be extra cautious after drinking *any* amount of alcohol. This is no easy task—most people will believe they are no different now than when completely sober. Sadly, these are the same people who cry, "Everything happened so fast—I didn't have time to react!" In truth, their reflexes were numbed and they weren't paying attention in the first place.

8. If there is any question in your mind about whether or not you should drive, then by all means exercise your options:
    A. Call a taxi.
    B. Call a friend or relative for a ride.
    C. Walk to a bus stop and ride.
    D. Walk home.

E.   Sleep in your car.

F.   Walk to a motel and take a room for the night.

Try anything—but don't make a "live bomb" out of your car by trying to drive it home. Some of these options may seem a little "inconvenient", but have you ever seen the inside of a jail—or a morgue? Go take a look sometime. You won't like it!

WHEN THE SIREN COMES ON

Now, supposing you have done everything just right, you haven't broken any laws or smashed into anyone, and the flashing red lights come on behind you anyway? (Maybe a taillight is out—or your registration tags have expired.) If a cop is approaching your car and he sees you fire up a cigarette, he's probably going to assume that you have been drinking. It's very common for a drinking driver to start smoking cigarettes immediately after being stopped as an attempt to mask the odor of alcohol on the breath. For the record, quickly popping breath mints or dousing your mouth with a pocket breath spray will have the same effect: a tip-off to the cop that you feel you have something to hide.

Don't be dumb enough to be caught with an open container of alcohol that can be seen anywhere inside your car. It will create more reason to arrest you and probably add a second charge and a bigger fine.

You should always keep your driver's license in a convenient place in your wallet so that it will be very easy to find and remove. Your driver's license can become quite elusive after you've had a few drinks. You don't want that sneaky devil with the badge to tell the judge that you were so drunk you couldn't even find your driver's license!

WHAT TO EXPECT IF
YOU ARE STOPPED

Let's discuss some of the things you can expect from the police after you have presented your driver's license and the officer suspects you have been drinking:

You will be asked to exit your vehicle and walk to a safe location—probably on the nearby shoulder or sidewalk. At this point, the officer may want to give you a balance test. *[NOTE: If you refuse to do a balance test or take a blood test, your refusal will be seen as an attempt to hide something. Your refusal will later be used against you in court. Not to mention that it will confirm the suspicion in the officer's mind that you are under the influence—and you know it. Also, your driving privilege may be suspended by the DMV just for refusing to take a blood-alcohol test.]*

When you're getting out to do a balance test or just to talk to the officer, be as cool and calm as you can. This is not a good time to joke around. If you are being funny, you might be considered drunk.

Wait for the officer to tell you step by step what to do. You should not volunteer any more conversation than is necessary to communicate when answering questions. The officer will do most of the talking. Just do exactly what you are told to do, nothing more, nothing less. He is going to be listening and watching every move you make. Just try to relax and cooperate.

Following instructions is part of the test. If you try to get ahead of him he will realize that you have taken balance tests before—which will cause him to believe you are driving under the influence *once again.*

QUICK TEST BEFORE DRIVING

If you want to test your own abilities prior to getting behind the wheel and after a few drinks, try saying the alphabet smoothly without making a mistake ... *if you cannot recite the alphabet quickly, smoothly, without hesitating, stumbling, leaving out letters or having to start over, DON'T DRIVE!*

You should see the look on the face of a college graduate after he or she has made two or three unsuccessful attempts at reciting the alphabet without transposing or leaving out a couple of letters. Now **that's** funny.

It's surprising how many people will have to use the jingle from the alphabet song and actually **sing** the alphabet during the test.

I recently stopped a well-dressed, wealthy-looking man because his Lincoln Town Car was weaving slightly within its lane. He had been drinking a little, so I gave him a balance test. He performed very well. I decided to ask him to recite the alphabet. Prior to doing this I always ask how high the person has gone in school. (You would be surprised at some of the answers to that question.) This man said he was a college graduate. Off-handedly, I then asked if he knew the alphabet. He hesitated, then said, "Yes, I think so." I asked him how many letters does it have. He said, "Thirty-six, I think." I told him I thought it had only 26 letters. He replied quite confidently, "No. No, I'm sure it has thirty-six!" I thought maybe he knew something I didn't and told him to go ahead and recite all 36 of them for me. He started in, "A—B—C—D—uh? D?—uh? D?—uh..." He stopped and looked at me, then at my partner, scratched his head and said, "I guess I don't know the alphabet." He then admitted that he had only been to the 6th grade. The situation was funny, yet sad. The man really could not recite something as basically necessary to his education as the alphabet. (Incidentally, he was not arrested.)

WHAT WILL GET YOU ARRESTED

Just because you have been drinking doesn't mean you are automatically going to jail. The officer is going to have to make a decision. He is going to try to figure out approximately how much you have had to drink and if that amount has affected your ability to operate a motor vehicle safely. His decision is going to be based on the following:

1. Your driving.

2. Your speech.

3. The odor of an alcoholic beverage on your breath or person.

4. The condition of your eyes (e.g. blood-shot, eyelids at "half-mast").

5. Your attitude (e.g. belligerent, combative, over-cooperative or cautious, etc.—or a sudden change in attitude from one extreme to another).

6. Your physical appearance (e.g. hair messed up, food spilled on your dress, no shoes, fly open, etc.).

7. The officer's personal expertise in being able to detect the sometimes subtle characteristics of a person who has been drinking.

WHADDAYA MEAN, CRAWLING A
STRAIGHT LINE DOESN'T COUNT?

8. Your ability to perform a simple balance test:

    Have a friend put you through this and observe your performance the next time you have had a few drinks. Then try it on your friend. It's best to do it sober first so you will have an indication of how much you have been affected. The test goes something like this:

    A. Stand at attention, arms down, head tilted back, eyes closed. You should be able to stand still without swaying back and forth or from side to side.

    B. From position A: arms outstretched, you should be able to touch the tip of your nose with the tip of your index fingers one at a time. If you hit your bridge or upper lip, you're out ("under the influence").

    C. With head level, eyes open and leg straight, raise your left foot 6 inches off the floor. Hold for 10 seconds without dropping your foot. Now do the right foot.

    D. Walk in a straight line for about 10 steps, heel against toe. Turn briskly and repeat in the opposite direction. You may not stagger, space your steps or stumble while turning.

If you do not excel on this balance test, **do not drive!** Practicing this test frequently will not buy you anything. You won't be able to fool an experienced police officer, nor will you be able to fool the alcohol in your bloodstream by attempting to perform this test as if you were sober. *But I strongly suggest that you use this test after a few drinks to help determine whether or not you should drive.*

ADDITIONAL ASSISTANCE

To further assist you in determining your blood-alcohol content, there are reference charts available from police agencies, departments of motor vehicles, and anti-drunk driving organizations. Please get one and use it as an additional tool to help keep you and others alive.

This is only one example of what these charts will tell you: If you weigh 150 pounds and have consumed four drinks in one hour, your blood-alcohol content will be at a .10% or higher. (Jail time.) What is a "drink"? A 12 ounce beer, a 4 ounce glass of wine or a 1 1/4 ounce shot of 80 proof liquor (either solo or mixed).

GO TO JAIL — DO NOT COLLECT $200

If you have failed the balance test and the other mentioned factors are against you, an arrest will follow. You will be handcuffed and placed into the patrol car. You will be advised of your rights and offered a chemical test to determine the alcoholic content of your blood. In California, you must choose either a blood, breath or urine test. Should you choose blood or urine, you will be transported to a medical facility where blood will be drawn from your arm or a urine sample collected. Either will be mailed to a laboratory for analysis. Meanwhile, you will be presumed "under the influence" and will be booked and jailed.

If a breath test is chosen, you will be transported to the jail facility and asked to blow into a machine which provides immediate results. If you fail, you will then be booked and confined to the jail for at least 4 or 5 hours until you are sober.

DRIVING AND DRUGS

Much of the same or similar procedures are used when arresting people for driving under the influence of drugs.

[NOTE: It should be emphasized here that even drugs prescribed by your doctor can cause your driving to be affected. That's why pharmacists use the warning labels stating something to the effect of "This drug may cause drowsiness—do not operate a car or any dangerous machinery." Some over-the-counter drugs can affect your driving, and consequently, you can be arrested for driving under the influence of LEGAL prescription or nonprescription drugs.

Mixing drugs and alcohol creates a synergistic effect. This means that combining the two often causes the effects of the drug and alcohol to magnify and intensify within the body, doubling or tripling the level of intoxication and resulting in a loss of coordination.]

If you are arrested for driving under the influence of any drug, including, but not limited to marijuana, cocaine or heroin, the sequence of events is similar to drunk driving. First, the officer observes unusual or erratic driving. Second, a field sobriety test or balance test is administered. If your eyes are too dilated or are pin-pointed, drugs may be suspected. If your speech is too fast or slow—or if no alcoholic beverage is smelled or otherwise evidenced, drugs may be suspected (needle marks on the body may be a giveaway).

Some officers are specially trained as "drug recognition experts". One of these may be called upon to make a more positive determination of drug usage.

The suspect may then be subjected to a blood or urine test or both for laboratory analysis to ascertain the existence of a specific drug in the body.

If drugs are found in the vehicle, additional charges are made against this person. He or she will then be booked-in at the jail facility the same as alcohol-related drunk drivers.

*   *   *

CAN THE POLICE SEARCH
YOUR CAR?

I have often been asked if the police have the arbitrary right to search a vehicle? (Or is it considered "trespassing" if they do not have a specific warrant?) A general answer is NO—the police cannot search your vehicle without "probable cause". What are some examples of "probable cause"?

A.   *An odor of beer or another alcoholic beverage emanating from within a vehicle, coupled with the observance of spilled liquid on the floorboards, or a paper sack about the size of a six-pack.*

B.   *A strong odor of burning marijuana emanating from within the vehicle and a strange-looking half-burned "cigarette" protruding from an ashtray.*

C.   *The mere observance of the neck of a whiskey bottle protruding from between or under a seat.*

D.   *An empty holster or shell casing on the seat or floorboards.*

If there are no specific observations—only a mere suspicion of a violation or crime—then the police need either your permission or a search warrant. But, you've seen most of this on TV anyway, haven't you?

Just remember this: the courts have said, "The eye cannot commit a trespass." So if I spot something that looks illegal in your car with my flashlight, I'm going after it. If I go after a bottle of beer and I accidentally find a bag of cocaine, you are in serious trouble!

* * *

Even as you read this, newer, tougher drunk driving laws are being written and enacted. A recently enacted law in California provides that if you have had three drunk driving convictions within the past seven years and are now being arrested, you will be charged with a felony.

IF ARRESTED, WHAT HAPPENS TO YOUR CAR?

If you are stopped by the police for driving under the influence and are subsequently arrested, obviously you will not be driving your car another inch. What happens to it?

A. If it is legally parked or can be legally parked close by, the officer may choose to lock it up and leave it at the scene.

B. The vehicle could also be released to a sober passenger with a valid driver's license.

C.   But most likely, (especially if the vehicle is a traffic hazard or if you have valuables inside), a tow truck will be summoned by radio to the scene and the vehicle will be impounded and stored at the owner's expense.

* * *

Once again, the preceding information in no way means that I condone, endorse or encourage anyone to drink and drive. I wish to take this opportunity to make myself perfectly clear, both as a citizen and a law enforcement officer. My advice is, if you have had one or more drinks of beer, wine, whiskey or any alcoholic beverage—or are taking any drugs, prescription or otherwise, DO NOT attempt to operate any vehicle, motorized or otherwise, on or off the highways! Instead use one of the options listed on pages 66-67.

You will notice throughout this book that my advice is always to obey the laws. The only way to eliminate drunk or drinking drivers is to eliminate alcohol. Since this is not going to happen, the alternative is stricter enforcement of existing laws by the police and the courts to help make people more aware. Hopefully, they will become more cautious and the effect will be a reduction in fatalities. And more hopefully, that will be enough to keep someone you know or love from being injured or killed by someone who abuses alcohol and their privilege to drive.

TRAFFIC ACCIDENTS

What do traffic accidents have to do with traffic tickets?

In most states you can and probably will receive a traffic ticket if you are found to be at fault in a traffic accident. You may be ticketed at the scene or you could receive one in the mail a week or two after the investigation from the police agency involved.

The word "accident" is probably a misnomer. The correct word to describe a so-called traffic accident is "collision". The reason for this is that most collisions are not merely *accidents* or an *act of nature* or an *act of God*. In most cases, a collision occurs as the result of a violation of a traffic law—whether intentional or *unintentional*. For instance, you reach over to adjust your radio and in that moment of inattention to the road, you "run" a stop sign and broadside another car. You may not have intended to do so, but you just violated your state law that requires you to stop for all stop signs.

If the police report reveals that you have violated a traffic law which caused or even contributed to a traffic collision, you may be cited (ticketed).

BUT OFFICER, IT'S NOT MY FAULT! THAT TREE IS
ILLEGALLY *PLANTED* IN A RED ZONE!

BE PREPARED—BE CAREFUL—
BE COOL—BE QUIET

The bad news here is that you are probably not going to be able to talk your way out of any ticket that is issued as a result of such a collision. So, what *can* you do to make your situation as positive as is possible? Here are some suggestions:

1. *Always carry a pad and pencil in your vehicle.*

2. *Identify and be able to describe the other car and driver involved in your collision as soon as possible. Get a license number and WRITE IT DOWN!*

3. *Try to stay cool and calm—and do not become engaged in an argument with the other driver(s) or passengers.* Too late to cry over spilled milk now.

4. If possible, *try to protect cars and passengers from any further collisions or damage.*

5. *Provide assistance to other parties.*

6. *Avoid discussing the collision with anyone except the police.*

7. It's okay to explain to the police your version of the events leading up to the collision, *but you shouldn't make incriminating statements* such as, "Gee, I'm sorry, it's all my fault." The police are experts at determining who is at fault. Let them decide.

8. **Don't leave the scene before providing the other driver or the police with your driver's license, vehicle and insurance information.**

9. **Make sure you get the other driver's (and passenger's, if any) information:** *driver's license, insurance information, license plate number (check the plates to determine if their car is under current registration!)*

10. **Make notes on the EXACT damage to the other vehicle.** (It's funny how "mystery" dents and additional damage will sometimes miraculously occur if it is later determined that the accident is your fault.) The same applies to injuries—so **find out if anyone is hurt and to what extent.**

11. **Phone your insurance company after leaving the scene.** They will help you with any further details. *[NOTE: The **exception** would be if you feel your situation is **serious** and you may be in some kind of trouble. If this is the case, you should consult with an attorney prior to talking to **anyone** else!]*

12. **Always wear your seat belt.** In most states, failure to do so *automatically* results in a ticket.

In conclusion, should you become the unfortunate participant or victim of a traffic collision, don't panic. Just heed the above common sense advice and keep the odds of success and survival in your favor. Let the police determine who is at fault. They will do so based on physical evidence found at the scene of the accident more than on statements made by you or any other driver or witness. ***Drive carefully!***

✳✳✳✳✳✳✳✳✳✳✳✳✳✳✳✳✳✳✳✳✳✳✳✳✳✳✳✳✳

Do you think this woman had a good excuse for hit and run? Here are the details: A pick-up truck was being pushed by three young men who were trying to get it restarted after it stalled in the street. It was after dark and they had neglected to turn on the vehicle's lights. While they were pushing from both sides, along came a car which rear-ended the truck. There were no injuries, but the 50-year-old female driver of the car immediately got out and fled down a residential street. (In law enforcement circles, this is known as posting "foot bail".) On my arrival, two deputy sheriffs were already on the scene and one of them had found the driver of the car hiding in some bushes about a half-a-block away. He was walking her, handcuffed, toward my patrol car. She was wearing a white uniform dress and her legs and shoes were literally covered with human excrement. She told me she was a nurse and had been caring for an invalid in his home. Earlier she had taken a strong laxative and had consumed "several" drinks while "babysitting" the man. She was driving home and, when she struck the rear of the pick-up, everything inside her body suddenly let go. It was just awful. She said she couldn't face anyone in that condition so she ran away. (She was subsequently arrested for drunk driving and transported to jail seated on a plastic blanket on my right front seat.)

✳✳✳✳✳✳✳✳✳✳✳✳✳✳✳✳✳✳✳✳✳✳✳✳✳✳✳✳✳

BE PREPARED: PERSONAL EXPERIENCE

I was the victim of the following traffic collision. I believe that explaining the details will help to illustrate why I have advised you to carry a pad and pencil in your vehicle at all times:

I was off duty in my own personal car with my wife and son. It was around 8:00 p.m. and we had been shopping. I was stopped in the left turn pocket at a signal controlled intersection waiting for the red light to turn green. I heard an engine racing and saw a young man in a souped-up car preparing to turn left onto my street. He was also stopped at this same intersection to my right on the cross street waiting for his green light. He got his green light and began burning his rear tires as he accelerated across the intersection while trying to turn left at the same time. He lost control of his car and started sliding sideways. He was still accelerating when his car straightened out and lurched forward, smashing into my left front wheel and fender. His engine stalled on impact. The left front of my car was caved in and my door jammed shut, preventing me from being able to get out. My immediate thoughts were to identify the driver and get his license number in case he decided to leave the scene. I took a long look at his face as he was quickly restarting his car.

Sure enough, as my wife and I were exiting through her door, the other driver sped away down the street behind me. I had grabbed the pen and pad I keep in my glove compartment and wrote down his license number before he could disappear around the corner. I phoned the city police from an adjacent gas station, then returned to my own disabled car to wait for the police.

After about 15 minutes and just before the police arrived, I saw a couple of guys crossing into the street looking my car over. I recognized one of them as the other driver who had hit my car. When the policeman arrived, I asked him to obtain some identification from this "bystander". At first, the guy refused to ID himself saying, "Why? I'm not part of this! I don't have to show you anything!" He finally produced a driver's license at the policeman's insistence. The policeman called it in along with the license number I gave him and his dispatcher radioed back that the name of this "bystander" was the same as the registered owner of the car that had hit mine. It turned out that he had gone to a friend's house and had come back to the scene in his friend's car to see what he had done. (He had no intention of identifying himself. He was subsequently arrested for drunk driving and hit and run.) If I hadn't identified the driver and written down his license number, I would have been out of luck. I wouldn't have recognized him when he returned to the scene. As it turned out, he ended up paying for all my damages without the benefit of insurance on his car at the time.

HEY, LET'S FACE IT, JUDGIE—THIS COP IS A NITWIT!

SEE YOU IN COURT

Suppose you did everything just right and you and the cop are good friends now but you still ended up with a ticket. At this point, perhaps you are feeling down—feeling defeated. Well, chin up—you've only lost *one* round—you haven't lost the fight *yet*. You still have **one more chance** to 'talk your way out of a traffic ticket'!

If you do get a ticket and you feel that it was not justified, all is not lost. We still have a court system that is free for you to use. If you don't know how to use it, you can ask the clerk at the court. Or, you can go to a police station and ask for a supervisor and see if he would be so kind as to steer you in the right direction. If the violation is **serious** and you feel you need an expert, the Yellow Pages of your phone book will list several attorneys. Try to find one that has had experience in dealing with traffic laws. Not all attorneys do. It's always best to talk to a specialist.

IMPORTANCE OF ATTITUDE

I'm not going to go into the exact procedures for clearing a ticket or for pleading guilty or not guilty as they may vary from state to state or court to court.

But let's assume you have plead **not guilty** and you are now standing in front of the judge telling your side of the story. What should be your attitude toward the judge and the officer—and your demeanor in the courtroom? Again, speaking in human terms only, the judge's first impression of you is going to be positive or negative according to what you are wearing. Therefore, **dress up a little**. It's better to be over-dressed than to look as if you don't care. His or her second positive or negative impression of you is going to be when you start speaking.

Don't forget, the judge is a representative of the same judicial system that the officer is and *if you show contempt for the police, you are also indirectly showing contempt for the judge— BOTH represent the law*. A judge is supposed to make decisions objectively based on the information and evidence presented to him—and for the most part he will. But judges are not robots. They are human beings like you. They have dreams, desires, ambitions, problems, fears and prejudices. Some of their decisions are based on these things.

Even if the ticketing officer was discourteous, ignorant or just plain stupid, you can tell his sergeant but not the judge. The *officer's attitude* has no bearing on the law you are being accused of violating. So, **stick with the facts**. It is okay to tell the judge you think the officer probably felt he was doing his job when he wrote you the ticket, but, "I feel the officer made an honest mistake or error in judgement and this is why..."

Much of the same information I listed in the **DO**s and **DON'T**s Chapter for dealing with the officer who stopped you will apply in the court-room when you are talking to the judge.

MENTAL PREPARATION

The key to "beating" a ticket in the courtroom is **preparation**.

I am assuming you have decided not to hire an attorney to defend you. If you ever wanted to *be* an attorney, now is your chance. You need to put your mind in the frame of an attorney's. It doesn't really matter if your trial is to be before a jury or a judge only. Ask yourself what an attorney would do or say if he or she were going to defend your case.

Okay, what would an attorney do? Answer: **make lots of notes.**

RETURNING TO THE "SCENE OF THE CRIME"

A trip back to the scene of the alleged violation would be helpful—if it is safe or legal to do so. For instance, in California it would not be legal to stop on the freeway unless it was under emergency conditions.

I can't stress enough the importance of **photographs**! Take photos of things at the scene—like the roadway, any signs or markings that may be relevant or applicable. *[NOTE: written confirmation of posted signs, or their absence—or repair conditions can be obtained through the city or county department having jurisdiction over them.]* If there are any large physical obstructions or objects that may have obscured the officer's view, these should be photographed.

If safe and legal, measurements of the roadway and distances involved should be obtained.

Any witnesses should be questioned, their statements obtained, and ask them to appear with you. But be careful that your witness is not so anxious to help you that he or she starts making up things in court that were not actually seen or heard. This may become apparent and will work against you.

NOTES, NOTES AND MORE NOTES

Going back to the time the ticket was actually written, *it is advantageous for you to make some notes immediately after the officer leaves or as soon as it is convenient without letting too much time pass.* Notes concerning the alleged violation are best written while the details are fresh in your mind. In making notes, answer some basic questions: Who, what, where, when, why and how?

You can't always think clearly enough to notice *all* of these things, but try to obtain answers to some of the following:

1. What is the officer's name? (it should be on the ticket)

2. Did he have a partner?

3. Which officer was driving?

4. At what point did you first notice the patrol car?

5. Who was in your car at the time?

6. What was the condition of the roadway? (holes, ruts, construction, smooth, asphalt, concrete, wet, dry, slippery, icy, etc.)

7. What were the "light" conditions? (broad daylight, dusk, pitch black—no moon, sun rising and glaring in officer's eyes, dim or bright street lights, etc.)

8. What were the traffic conditions? (heavy, moderate, or light)

9. What type of vehicles were near you at the time and what effect, if any, did they have on your violation?

10. What were the weather conditions? (cool, sunny, cloudy, hot, windy, rain, snow, etc.)

11. What direction(s) were you and the patrol car traveling at the time? (north, west, south, east)

12. Were there any permanent or temporary traffic signs posted just prior to your being stopped?

* * *

The purpose of obtaining and preparing all the information humanly possible is:

1. *The officer is going to tell his side of the story. If you notice any errors while the officer is testifying, point these out to the judge. He or she is going to wonder if the cop really saw as much as he says.*

2. *You will have a chance to ask the officer some questions. The more questions he is unable to answer accurately, the weaker his case appears to be.*

3. *You will have a chance to tell your side of the story. Your story will appear believable if you sound as if you know exactly what you are talking about.*

4. *The officer will have a chance to ask you questions. If you can answer them accurately, the judge will be impressed with your knowledge and memory.*

PLAYING THE ROLE OF LAWYER

Your case usually does not come up in court for a couple of weeks or months. You have all that time to prepare your case and anticipate questions that might be asked of you. The officer, in the meantime, has written many more tickets and his memory of specific details in your case may have faded significantly.

If at all possible, I strongly suggest that you sit in on a traffic court session before your hearing date. This will help to familiarize you with the specific court procedures in advance.

Make your list of specific questions to ask the officer **before** arriving in court. What kind of questions should you ask the officer? **Very specific questions.** For example:

1. Where was your patrol car when you first noticed my car, Officer?

2. How far was your car from mine? (Get specific—how many feet? If you are a good mathematician, you can use his figures to calculate and see if it was even *possible* for him to have seen you, accelerated to the necessary speed, and paced your car adequately prior to stopping you in the given distances.)

3. Officer, did you notice if there were any other vehicles in the area at the time?

4. Did you notice if *all* the signals at the intersection were working properly?

5. What were the weather conditions at the time?

6. Was traffic light or heavy?

7. How wide was the roadway?

8. What color, make, model, etc., was the other car involved?

The list goes on according to the details of your own situation. ***Make sure the questions are related to your case.*** And ***don't argue*** as the officer is answering the questions. Just take notes. If he doesn't answer the questions accurately, you can point it out to the judge later.

If the officer's case is no stronger than yours, and the judge sees that you have gone to a lot of trouble to prepare your case, he may make a decision in your favor for almost no other reason. I've seen it happen.

[NOTE: It should be pointed out here that in many courtrooms, the officer will be represented by a prosecuting attorney. This attorney will be asking you the kinds of questions I have advised you to prepare for in this chapter. Find out prior to your trial date if the court into which you are cited operates this way. If it turns out that there will be a prosecuting attorney against you as well as the officer, you may want to hire your own attorney to defend you if you feel your case is serious enough to justify the cost of doing so.]

IF YOU'RE LUCKY

What if you have done all that preparation, have numerous photos, 10 pages of notes and measurements and a convincing list of questions and the officer does not show up on your trial date? There is a good possibility, depending somewhat on the circumstances, that the judge will look at you and say, "Mrs. Jones, the officer was unable to be here today due to illness. Your case is dismissed." It happens.

The criminal justice system is run by people. We all know that people make mistakes. That's one of the reasons we needed the system in the first place. People also make mistakes within the system. These mistakes are often the reason why you are found "not guilty" in court.

* * *

In summary, there are many factors which can influence the outcome of your case (your attitude, memory, persistence, and preparedness—plus visibility, road and weather conditions at the "scene of the crime"—the seriousness of the violation, etc.). If all or most of these factors are in your favor, your chances of 'beating' a ticket in court are greatly enhanced.

✻✻✻✻✻✻✻✻✻✻✻✻✻✻✻✻✻✻✻✻✻✻✻✻✻✻✻✻✻✻✻

The following excuse was used in a courtroom during a jury trial on a speeding ticket. I know the story because it was my own case. I had written the ticket in question. The defendant told the judge, "Your Honor, my motorcycle does not have a speedometer, but I have been riding motorcycles for over 20 years. I know whenever I am going over 25 miles per hour because my eyes will start watering. When the officer wrote me a ticket for 40 in a 25 zone, I couldn't have been going over 25 because my eyes were not watering at the time." Apparently, the judge was not particularly impressed with this excuse. He leaned forward over his bench, glaring down at the defendant over the top of his glasses and said, "Now tell me, Mr. Jones, how closely are your eyeballs calibrated? What I mean is, are your eyeballs calibrated to within plus or minus two miles per hour? ... Or five miles per hour? Because I know the officer's speedometer is calibrated very closely. I'm just trying to compare his speedometer to your eyeballs." Mr Jones didn't know how to reply to this question. I think he just exercised his right to remain silent. It was all I could do to keep from laughing. (I think the jury felt the same way as I did because Mr. Jones was found guilty very quickly.)

✻✻✻✻✻✻✻✻✻✻✻✻✻✻✻✻✻✻✻✻✻✻✻✻✻✻✻✻✻✻✻

PLAYING YOUR LAST CARD

In some states there is a last, last resort—an option to avoid having your traffic violation appear on your driving record at the department of motor vehicles: **Traffic School**.

Traffic School is usually a one-day classroom session instructed by a police officer or other qualified individual. The theory behind Traffic School is that, once attended, you will be a more informed and consequently a better driver. As a reward for becoming more informed, the court will not forward your conviction to the DMV. There may still be a fine involved, however, to help defray the cost of operating the school (or there may be a fine and admission fee, both).

Traffic School is only made available to drivers with relatively clean driving records. To ascertain the availability of Traffic School and whether or not you qualify, contact the specific court into which you are cited.

Obviously, the more violations which appear on your driving record, the greater the possibility of higher insurance rates or having your driver's license suspended by the motor vehicle department in your state. So, if you're in court and it looks as though you are not going to be able to talk your way *out* of the violation, if at all possible, talk your way *into* Traffic School.

[NOTE: Be sure to check into the procedure beforehand. Some courts will only allow Traffic School if you enter a "guilty" plea at the outset. In other words, if you plead "innocent" and lose your case, you can't then ask for Traffic School as an alternative.]

ARE YOU SURE I WAS SPEEDING, OFFICER?

SUMMARY

The purpose of this book has been to provide the reader with a traffic officer's perspective in order to clarify and hopefully eliminate misunderstandings. This clarification should help to put the odds more in your favor when dealing with the police.

Throughout this book there has prevailed a key factor to consider if one is to "talk your way out of a traffic ticket". This factor, in many cases, will determine the failure or success of the contact between you and the law enforcement officer who stops you for a traffic violation. *This factor is human relations and behavior.* The behavior you exercise during a traffic stop through your words and actions is a direct result of your attitudes or preconceived ideas about the police.

It has been my observation over the years that too many people do not understand the true function of the police. In most instances, the average person cannot understand a police officer's perspective toward law enforcement unless he himself had been involved in enforcing the law in some capacity.

103

Not only are there the verbal exchanges between you and the officer to consider, but there are other specific "courtesies"or "gestures" you can do to make his job easier. By making his job easier you help create a more positive and safe environment for the both of you. [Refer back to the **DO**s **& DON'T**s Chapter for these specifics.] If there is any chance for you to talk your way out of a traffic stop situation, it is going to depend largely on the most positive environment that's within your power and ability to create. Knowledge is power. Hopefully, this book has provided you with the necessary knowledge to do and say the right things when you see the flashing red lights in your rear-view mirror.

If you are going to use an excuse for your driving actions, just remember, as discussed in the **COP - OUTS** Chapter, make it good—no, make it *great,* or it won't work. Don't forget, we've already heard most of them!

If, for some reason, all else fails and you still feel that you honestly did not break any laws, you still have the option of entering a "not guilty" plea in court. But don't make a fool of yourself by appearing in court without a sound defense. Just telling the judge you feel you are not guilty won't cut it. You have to be able to demonstrate or substantiate *how* and *why* you are not guilty. Remember, as I told you in the **SEE YOU IN COURT** Chapter, the "key" to fighting a ticket in court is *preparation.* Take notes, take photos and, if possible, take measurements.

* * *

In life there are no guarantees. But there are ways to overcome obstacles and negative situations. You can only give it your best shot and hope to succeed. On the other hand, we all have responsibilities as citizens to do the right thing so as not to hurt others. If you have done something you know to be wrong, face the music. Stand up and show some character. ***Pay the fine and get on with your life.***

****

After seeing a car suddenly swerve to the dirt shoulder of the freeway, (it is illegal to stop along the freeway in California unless you have an emergency) I pulled in behind to see if I could be of assistance. As I approached the car on foot, I observed the driver in a liplock embrace with his female passenger. When I asked why he had stopped on a busy freeway he said, "Officer, this is my girlfriend. I just felt an overwhelming urge to kiss her!" Somehow I had difficulty applying the word "emergency" to his situation and I wrote him a ticket. I later made the mistake of telling my wife about the incident. She instantly became angry with me and accused me of being "unromantic". Is there any justice in the world?

****

EPILOG

If, after reading this book, you find you have been ticketed anyway, do not be discouraged. Look at the positive side, getting tickets can be fun! Think of all the new people you will meet. You now have a *friend* on the police force. You will get to meet the clerk at the courthouse. You may get to know the District Attorney by his first name. And I'm sure you always wanted to meet someone as powerful as a judge!

Just kidding. But I would like to add one thing. If you did do something *intentionally* that caused a hazardous traffic situation where someone could have been injured or killed, then kindly disregard the information I just gave you and accept the ticket—you obviously need one. And, if you are basically a safe driver who made a minor mistake and got caught, I hope you won't hold it against us. We're really on your side, you know.

BUT DOES IT REALLY WORK?

During the process of putting this book together, I gave a copy of my notes to a friend of mine. He is not involved in law enforcement so I thought he might give me an objective viewpoint and hopefully non-biased opinion on this information.

About two weeks after reading my notes he was stopped by the local police. Two officers on patrol *had seen him enter a signal controlled intersection at about the same time the light had changed from yellow to red. He told the officers he was sure the signal was still yellow when he entered the intersection. They insisted it was definitely red. My friend, who usually has a hot temper, was about to challenge the officers' eyesight and suggest they have it examined when his mind flashed back to my manuscript notes that said "**Don't argue!**" He decided to test my advice and told the officers that they were probably right, he had a lot on his mind and perhaps he did misjudge the signal change.*

Coincidentally, my older son's fiancé was at the same intersection and saw my friend go through the signal. When she stopped by my house a few minutes later, she told me he had to have gotten a ticket because the light was clearly red and the policemen saw it plain as day.

About an hour later, my friend called me from his home. "Hey David, guess what?" His voice was a mixture of exhilaration and disbelief. "I just talked my way out of a traffic ticket!"

P.S. Here's hoping YOU enjoy a lifetime of safe, ticket free driving!

TEST?

I have found that most serious "How To" books are all work and no play. To lighten things up a little, I submit the following test—but don't worry, no matter how you do, you won't fail!

1. If an officer asks you for your driver's license, you should:
   A. *Cry.*
   B. *Laugh.*
   C. *Plead insanity.*
   D. *Accelerate.*

2. If you are in a 35 mph zone and your speed-ometer indicates 70, you should:
   A. *Get a new speedometer.*
   B. *Pick up your car phone and report yourself to the police.*
   C. *Ignore the siren.*
   D. *Make sure your window is rolled up so the wind doesn't mess up your hair.*

3. If you are at a railroad crossing and your car stalls on the tracks and a train is coming, you should:

   A. Fasten your seat belt.

   B. Turn up the radio.

   C. Lock your doors.

   D. Get in the back seat.

4. You have just been told you are under arrest for drunk driving, you should:

   A. Request a second opinion.

   B. Promise never to drink another drop—not even water—ever again.

   C. Ask if you can "go to your room with no TV" instead.

5. You just drove through an intersection at 40 mph past a posted stop sign, you should:

   A. Feel guilty.

   B. Find a cop and ask for a ticket.

   C. Stop twice for the next one.

   D. Back up and try again.

6. You're late and you hastily back out of a diagonal parking stall broadsiding a police car, you should:

   A. Pray.

   B. Quickly slide over to the right and pretend you're a passenger.

   C. Offer to buy a ticket to the Policeman's Ball.

7. You notice your left front tire is so thin you can almost see the air inside, you should:

    A. *Put it on the right rear so it won't be as noticeable.*

    B. *Drive fast so it will blow out and you can get a new one.*

    C. *"Retread" it by driving down a freshly tarred road.*

8. You are descending a long, steep grade and the brakes have just gone out of your brand new $50,000 motor home. There is a construction zone at the bottom. You should:

    A. *Rush back to the mini-kitchen and scarf down your "last meal".*

    B. *Call the salesman from the hospital and ask for your money back.*

    C. *Climb into one of the bunkbeds and pretend it's only a bad dream.*

    D. *Start traveling by air.*

9. Your mother-in-law phones you from the county jail. She has just been booked for drunk driving and assaulting a police officer. She needs bail. You should:

    A. *Fake a "bad connection".*

    B. *Go to the bank, take out a loan, leave for Hawaii.*

    C. *Break out the champagne and party hats.*

    D. *Test the police's sense of humor: try to bail her out with Monopoly money.*

10. You are driving the wrong way on the free-way. At first you thought everyone else was out of step. Now, you finally realize your mistake. You should:

A.   *Take pride in being a non-conformist.*

B.   *Quickly stop, shift gears and drive 55 mph in reverse.*

C.   *Stop your car. Get out and walk for the rest of your life.*

11. You are doing 60 mph in a residential zone. You suddenly notice the red lights of a police car in your rear view mirror directly behind you. You should:

A.   *Slam on your breaks and teach the cop a lesson.*

B.   *Slow down to 25 and hope the cop will forget.*

C.   *Act like you are doing nothing wrong and wave at him to pass around you.*

12. You are on your way home from visiting friends. It is 4:00 a.m. You are in a dense fog, visibility:10 feet. You should:

A.   *Be on the lookout for vampires.*

B.   *Drive 9 feet and stop. Drive 9 feet and stop. Drive 9 feet and stop. Etc.*

C.   *Make sure you keep wide awake—turn your radio on full blast!*

13. You're a passenger in a car. The driver just turned left instead of right (the wrong way on a one-way street) and plowed into another car. You should:

   A.   *Jump out and run for it.*

   B.   *Hide in the trunk until it all blows over.*

   C.   *Exclaim, "I've got better things to do!" and start hitchhiking.*

   D.   *If the other driver tries to get your name, start drooling.*

14. You are traveling at the 55 mph speed limit and are being tailgated by an 18 wheeler, two feet from your back bumper. You should:

   A.   *Turn off the ignition and catch a "free ride".*

   B.   *Honk: 3 short, 3 long, 3 short (SOS) until you are rescued.*

   C.   *Pop open your trunk lid so he can't see you and take pleasure in how frightened you are.*

   D.   *Show him the nice manicure on your middle finger.*

HAPPY MOTORING!

TITLES BY CCC PUBLICATIONS
—NEW BOOKS—

NEVER A DULL CARD
THE ABSOLUTE **LAST CHANCE** DIET BOOK
HUSBANDS FROM HELL
HORMONES FROM HELL (The Ultimate *Women's* Book!)
FOR **MEN** ONLY (How To Survive Marriage)
THE Unofficial WOMEN'S DIVORCE GUIDE
HOW TO TALK YOUR WAY OUT OF A TRAFFIC TICKET
WHAT DO WE DO NOW?? (The Complete Guide For All New
    Parents Or Parents-To-Be)
THE SUPERIOR PERSON'S GUIDE TO EVERYDAY
    IRRITATIONS
YOUR GUIDE TO CORPORATE SURVIVAL
GIFTING RIGHT (How To Give A Great Gift Every Time! For Any
    Occasion! And On Any Budget!)

—COMING SOON—

HOW TO **REALLY** PARTY!!!
THE GUILT BAG (Accessory Item)
THE PEOPLE WATCHER'S FIELD GUIDE
IT'S BETTER TO BE OVER THE HILL—THAN UNDER IT
WORK IS AN OCCUPATIONAL HAZARD
THE UGLY TRUTH ABOUT MEN
THE BOTTOM HALF

—BEST SELLERS—

NO HANG-UPS (Funny Answering Machine Messages)
NO HANG-UPS II
NO HANG-UPS III
GETTING EVEN WITH THE ANSWERING MACHINE
HOW TO GET EVEN WITH YOUR EXes
HOW TO SUCCEED IN SINGLES BARS
TOTALLY OUTRAGEOUS BUMPER-SNICKERS
THE "MAGIC BOOKMARK" BOOK COVER (Accessory Item)

—CASSETTES—

NO HANG-UPS TAPES (Funny, Pre-recorded Answering Machine
    Messages With Hilarious *Sound Effects*) — In Male or Female Voices
Vol. I: GENERAL MESSAGES
Vol. II: BUSINESS MESSAGES
Vol. III: 'R' RATED MESSAGES
Vol. IV: SOUND EFFECTS ONLY
Vol. V: CELEBRI-TEASE (Celebrity Impersonations)